Holy Homework

PUTTING OUR INTERIOR FAITH
INTO EXTERIOR PRACTICE

FATHER BOB PAGLIARI, C.Ss.R., Ph.D.

Liguori
PUBLICATIONS
A Redemptorist Ministry

Imprimi Potest: Stephen T. Rehrauer, C.Ss.R., Provincial
Denver Province, the Redemptorists

Published by Liguori Publications, Liguori, Missouri 63057
Liguori Publications, a nonprofit corporation, is an apostolate of the Redemptorists
(Redemptorists.com).

Phone: 800-325-9521 *Web:* Liguori.org

Holy Homework: Putting Our Exterior Faith into Exterior Practice
Copyright © 2022 Robert Pagliari
ISBN 978-0-7648-2863-8
Library of Congress Control Number: 2022948725

Originally published by Catholic New York (cny.org),
1011 First Avenue, New York, New York 10022,
© 2018 Fr. Robert Pagliari, C.Ss.R., Ph.D.

Printed in the United States of America
26 25 24 23 22 / 5 4 3 2 1
First Edition

Cover design by Wendy Barnes.
Interior design by Leah Bossi

DEDICATION

To my parents, Albert and Lillian, and to my godmother, Linda—
my first teachers who instructed me in life's holiest homework:
the virtues of faith, hope, and love.
Thank you.

ACKNOWLEDGMENTS

My sincere thanks to the following friends for their support,
encouragement, and guidance:

Msgr. Patrick McCahill

Rev. John Vargas, C.Ss.R.

Rev. Min Seo Park

Sr. Dolores Galantich, FDC

Sr. Janet Marchesani, OP

Margaret Shea and the members of the deaf community

Rev. Richard L. Welch, C.Ss.R., JCD

Marsha Sinetar

Jeanie Ransom

John Papatsos

The Martini Family

The Colaguori Family

The Cratty Family

The Fitzsimmons Family

St. James' Parishioners

St. Michael's Parishioners

Patrick Alog, Cyrus Simcoe, John Harper, Glen Lewerenz,
and the incredible crew at Relevant Radio

John Woods, Edith Nagy, Leah Bossio, Matt Schiller,
and the super staffs of Catholic New York and Liguori Publications

God bless you all.

Fr. Robert Pagliari, C.Ss.R., Ph.D.

For more than forty years, Fr. Robert Pagliari has dedicated his life as a Redemptorist priest to an array of ministries, including teaching, preaching, parish administration, and editing manuscripts for Liguori Publications, Doubleday, and the Crossroad Publishing Company.

As a professor, he has taught in-class and online courses for undergraduate and graduate students at universities and seminaries in New York, Virginia, Florida, Connecticut, and Louvain, Belgium, where he served as chairman of the homiletics department at the American College. He completed a bachelor's degree in philosophy and master's degrees in speech, psychology, theology, and religious education. He is certified in computer programming and Gestalt psychotherapy and holds an earned doctorate in communication from the University of Denver. His published audio, video, workbook, and textbook collections titled *Fourteen Steps to Dynamic Preaching* appeared in English in 1993. The book was later purchased and translated by Spanish and Indonesian distributors.

Fr. Bob served on the board of directors for Heartsong Inc., a music and art therapy program for differently abled children. He conducted support groups for the parents of children with special needs and was appointed director of the Department for Persons with Disabilities for the Archdiocese of New York.

In 2002, he began writing a monthly online column for *Catholic New York*, the newspaper of the archdiocese. This book is a selection of those compositions. In 2004, he resumed teaching theology and communication courses for St. John's University. Relevant Radio welcomed him as a monthly guest to the broadcast of their *Morning Air* program in 2008.

In his spare time, Fr. Bob enjoys a leisurely round of golf.

Contents

Preface

The Origin of
Holy Homework

I owe a huge debt of gratitude to the woman who accosted me after a Sunday Mass in 2007. I did not know her name then and I still don't know her today. Here's what happened. On the Friday prior to the Sunday in question my college students had been grilling me about what they should study for the upcoming exams. I remember assigning several items of homework and assuring them that if they reviewed and prepared well they were likely to receive a good grade. Two days later as I was nearing the end of my homily I still had that college homework assignment fresh in my mind, and suddenly I heard myself adding a twist to my pulpit talk. I blurted out, "for HOMEWORK…" and then added a small task for the congregation to do which reinforced the point of my message.

As was my custom, I stood at the back of church as the folks were leaving and noticed one middle-aged woman hanging back as if deliberately waiting to speak with me. I was correct. When all the other worshippers had gone, she was still standing there with an obviously stern look on her face. As I offered her my hand and a friendly smile she asked if I had ever heard of branding. I shook my head no. Branding, she explained, is a marketing technique which helps people identify products easily and immediately.

She offered the example of Campbell's soups, which all shoppers can recognize the moment they enter the canned-goods aisle of any food store. I remained silent, nodded my head to indicate that I understood the concept but kept wondering why she was lecturing me about marketing strategies. Then she got to the point. She said adding homework to the end of my talk was poor branding. She claimed everyone has a negative reaction to "homework" and that I should never have used that word, especially in the context of a church sermon.

I thanked her for her point of view, which felt more like a dressing-down, and she turned on her heel and marched away without so much as an "if, and, or by your leave."

For the next five days I replayed her scolding over and over in my head. Then as I was putting the finishing touches on my homily for the subsequent weekend, I was suddenly struck with a happy compromise and possibly innovative twist to the chapter on branding in textbooks for the future.

The next Sunday at the end of my homily I paused for a moment and announced, "for HOLY homework…" then added a new task for the congregation to perform which would underscore the point of the Bible readings. Needless to say, I have attached holy homework assignments to all my homilies ever since.

In a nutshell, that is when and how *Holy Homework* was born. And although I have never read a volume on marketing, I heartily thank this courageous woman, whoever she is, for sparking a brand name that may fit alongside soups for those souls who don't mind taking home some additional nourishment after Sunday Mass.

Gratefully,
Fr. Bob Pagliari, C.Ss.R, Ph.D.

P. S.: For those who read this preface, and if you wouldn't mind an extra smidgen of "holy homework," please offer up a prayer on behalf of this angelic woman. I'll never forget whatshername, and I can't thank her enough for the branding she inspired.

Happy New Year

Lord,
help us resolve to be happier
and holier people this year!

A Miraculous Change in New Year's Resolutions

Three years ago, I was invited to a seminar that addressed issues related to the pastoral care of the sick. Although this educational update was intended primarily for hospital chaplains, all the members of the clergy were welcome, so I was happy to attend. Among the many informational items presented was a Harris poll that examined patients' attitude toward prayer. Our seminary training, of course, had prepared us for the fact that people who are ill expect to pray when a church member visits them. But what we discovered from the study was that most hospitalized patients would also welcome the opportunity to pray with their physicians, especially if they're scheduled for a surgical procedure.

I left the seminar wondering whether doctors, who appear to be more concentrated on physical healing than on metaphysical miracles, would be open to this idea. Then, just two weeks ago, I discovered a nationwide investigation of physicians that indicates how very open they would be to the idea. This survey, conducted by the Jewish Theological Seminary in New York City, reported that 74 percent of American doctors believe in miracles.

This finding is especially interesting since a separate national inquiry conducted by *Newsweek* found only 72 percent of the general public believed that people who face death in accidents could be saved by a miracle. Could it be that our health professionals have a stronger faith than some of their ailing clients?

When we think about New Year's resolutions, miracles rarely come to mind. The majority of Americans are content to make simple promises like exercising more or spending less time at the office. And that's what this month's resolutions should be: simple, straightforward, doable goals, not grandiose, superhuman aspirations. But then again, if every person in the world made this simple resolve: to treat those around them, those closest to them, with a little more kindness, a little more compassion, and a little more love, the global result would be more astounding than any medical miracle we could imagine.

Wishing you and yours a blessed new year filled with daily, simple miracles.

HOLY HOMEWORK

Once each week during the next four weeks, let's select a health-care professional—a doctor, nurse, dentist, pharmacist, etc.—and send an anonymous note to his or her office. This can be a brief, old-fashioned thank-you card with the promise of a prayer. No signature, no return address, just an out-of-the-blue, totally unexpected token of appreciation and Christian support to make that professional's day a little brighter. We may discover that miraculous resolutions can begin with us.

The New Year's FOG

When we hear the word *fog* in connection with the new year, what leaps to mind immediately? Is it trying to remember where we left our mobile phone after calling all those fellow revelers at the stroke of midnight? Is it trying to forget that yet another 365 days has sped past us in the blink of an eye? Is it trying to recall the inventory of resolutions we swore we would be faithful to last year, if only we could find that laundry list?

The phrase "New Year's FOG" does not refer to hangovers, aging, or regrets. However, it does relate to resolutions—but only three of them.

These resolutions are:

Forgiveness

Optimism

Gratitude, or "FOG" for short. So why should these virtues be among our top picks for New Year's resolutions?

1) There are only three items here, and in terms of resolutions, less is more. Research assures us that the fewer promises we pledge for the New Year, the more likely we will be to follow through on them.

2) These three items are good for other people. Some virtues are directed inward, like faith and hope, for example. But the nature of these three behaviors is outgoing rather than self-focused. We tell others we are sorry. We are upbeat when we are around others. We say "thank you" to others.

3) These three items are good for us too. Although science and religion rarely seem to join forces nowadays, the medical community has indicated that these three character traits in particular are especially healthy for us.

Besides the many psychological benefits that come from being forgiving, positive and grateful, there are physiological pluses as well. Apparently those who practice the FOG oaths also benefit from a reduction in blood pressure, an increase in daily energy reserves, and an improved immune system. Not to mention the many spiritual profits for the soul!

Holy Homework

Put aside the extensive number of resolutions that you were determined to begin this year. Instead, post the word FOG in three locations—at the top of the bathroom mirror, near the handle of the refrigerator door, and dangling from the rearview mirror in your car. Then get ready to enjoy a happier, healthier, and holier New Year.

Resolutions
for a New Year:
Pray More,
Worry Less

Praying more and worrying less in the new year may look like two separate resolutions but they are not. They are the twin scales in our human balance. If we increase praying, we will automatically decrease worrying. Do you want to feel more joyful, upbeat and optimistic, and less melancholic, miserable and dejected during the next twelve months? Then here is a great resolution for the New Year. Bring more religion into your life and into your heart.

Although it may appear ironic, the sciences, including the social sciences, are demonstrating that faith is actually very good for our physical and psychological health. For example, Gallup pollsters have conducted a number of surveys on the relationship between religious belief and emotional well-being. They asked Americans from every age group, gender, race, ethnicity, region of the country, socioeconomic status, marital status, and child-bearing status whether they had ever suffered from depression and the extent of their religious practices.

The results were amazing and statistically significant. While holding all of the above variables constant and based on an analysis of more than 550,000 respondents, the scientists discovered that people who are very religious are less likely to be diagnosed with depression over the course of their entire lifetime than people who are only somewhat religious or not religious at all.

What's the secret here? Well, there really is no secret. Going to church at Christmas and Easter may qualify you as a somewhat religious person, but those extra hours of sleep on Sunday mornings are not going to stave off the gloom and doom of the rest of the week. However, resolving to attend Mass on a regular basis, whether we feel like going or not, is the surer way to happiness and to heaven.

There is, of course, the additional generalizing effect that comes with happier emotional well-being, which is enjoying more robust physical health. How many times has our doctor cautioned us to cut out the stress in our lives? The link between psychological stress and digestive disorders, skin abrasions, heart disease, and even cancer has clearly been established by medical research. So boosting our faith benefits our minds and bodies as well.

HOLY HOMEWORK

If we are already very faithful in our church attendance, then this year's resolution is easy; just promise to keep doing the same. If we are not very regular, then we can determine to increase our participation at church this year and in the future. Our bodies and souls and emotions will feel better and be better if we do.

Happy New Year!

Lord, help us to forgive quickly
and forget completely
and love unconditionally.

When Love Is Blind
—and Deaf

Each February we celebrate Valentine's Day. So we can aptly ask, where is true love? I never thought I'd find a physical address to answer that question, but I did. Last month I attended a special Mass in a church on the Upper East Side of Manhattan led by a newly ordained priest who is deaf. From where I concelebrated, I was easily able to see the gestures, the hand movements, and the finger spelling of the priest's sign language.

If you have never attended a Mass for the deaf, I strongly recommend you take advantage of such an opportunity. The dimension of constant and total communication brings a depth and richness to the sacred liturgy that is uniquely and powerfully different from the traditional gestures and spoken words alone.

However, I didn't see the fullness of love inside the communion rail that day. Only when I glanced outside the railing, toward the nave of the church, did my peripheral vision catch sight of some constant activity coming from the congregation. In the first bench sat a young couple. They were in their late twenties or early thirties at most. The woman was looking intently into the sanctuary and signing rapidly, determined not to miss a single syllable of what was going on. In fact, she was signing what was being said from the pulpit and filling in the nonverbal pieces that most of us take for granted. For example, she would be signing parenthetical notes like:

"Now the priest is making the sign of the cross on his forehead."
"Now the priest is walking from the lectern back to the altar."
"Now the priest is washing his hands with water and drying them with a towel."

In every Mass for the deaf that I've attended, this type of running commentary is unnecessary. Deaf people can see what's going on in church as easily as anyone else. But then I noticed something different. The young man sitting beside the woman was cupping the fingertips of his left hand around the fingers and knuckles of her right hand while she was signing. His eyes were closed but his facial expressions indicated that he clearly understood the communication coming from the woman's hand.

The young man was not only deaf. He was also blind. That's why she was signing the commentary, so he could also "see" what was going on.

As I refocused my attention on the solemnity of the occasion, I couldn't help but wonder what it must be like to be deaf and blind. I traveled back in my memory to the first time I watched the classic movie about Helen Keller called *The Miracle Worker*. I remembered how the struggle between teacher and pupil led a little girl from savagery and isolation into civilization and communion. United Artists Studio created a happy-ending story of overcoming genetic dependency with American independence.

But that was Hollywood. This is New York. From that wooden pew in St. Elizabeth of Hungary Church there was no ninety-minute resolution into freedom. There was only love: focused and sensory, gentle and hidden, constant and generous love. This young deaf-blind man was far from independent. On the contrary, for every sliver of information that he received about the living world around him he was totally dependent on his companion. And not just on her ability to communicate what was going on around them, but on her integrity to convey the truth of it, and not some false exaggeration.

I found it difficult to fathom what it must be like to depend solely and absolutely for every sight and sound around me on the presence of another person's outstretched hand. Such a fragile bridge, such a solitary link to humankind, can only be bolstered by the bedrock of true love.

Where is love? There is love: not withdrawing an enabling hand from another hand stretching out for help; not abandoning another human being into a world of silent darkness, unable to see the lips that move, or hear the words that ask, "Where is love?"

HOLY HOMEWORK

For a full ten minutes, wear headphones without listening to music and keep your eyes closed for the duration. Become aware of what it would be like to live for the rest of your life as a person who is deaf and blind. Ask a family member or friend to tap you on the shoulder when the ten minutes are up. Then offer a prayer of support for all those who are disabled and for their caretakers. Follow that prayer with another prayer of thanksgiving for the gifts of sight, sound, and unconditional love you have received.

Happy Valentine's Day.

Can God Be
Our Valentine?

Can God be our valentine? Why not? Children write letters to Santa Claus. Kids leave their lost teeth underneath their pillows for the Tooth Fairy. So why shouldn't we compose a valentine for God? The answer is: it depends on our understanding of what Valentine's Day means. After all, this saint's feast has changed considerably over the years.

A Joyful Trading Among Youthful Groups

I don't know if elementary teachers still allow the swapping of these heart-shaped notes in class, but not so long ago children carried bags full of valentines to and from school on February 14. I have many fond memories of these colorful exchanges when I was a second-grader. But given the current climate in education where a six-year-old boy who kisses a girl's hand may be suspended for harassment, maybe we shouldn't be surprised if passing out valentines might be labeled as some form of stalking.

A Romantic Flirtation Between Two Adults

Judging from the candy, florists, and greeting card companies, we can see how the original idea behind this inclusive, jubilant children's celebration has gradually matured into an exclusive, come-hither allure between couples. Has the advertising industry beguiled us into an Adam and Eve enticement simply because it is financially more lucrative to solicit grownups? Has the noble valentine become commercially serpentine?

True Love

Diametrically opposed to the spiteful snake that tempted our first parents into falling, God wants to raise us up to an eternal life of happiness with him. Since love is the essence of God, he exists for one purpose only: to love. Everything God does—his creating, his forgiving, his saving, and his sanctifying, stems from love. Loving us is what God does best. And like the valentine card in the hand of a child, God's love is selfless and unconditional. God's love is not "too good to be true" but rather "too immense not to be imitated."

Can God Be Our Valentine?

The answer is: God already *is* our valentine because he already loves us by wanting only what's best for us. This is the true meaning of love, and it mirrors the motivation behind the first "love notes" distributed by St. Valentine himself. So perhaps the more accurate question during this month of sweets, scents, and sentiments is not whether God can be our valentine, but are we willing to be God's valentine in return?

HOLY HOMEWORK

Write a heartfelt note to God thanking him for his unrestricted, plentiful love and promising him that we will imitate this colossal caring toward at least one neighbor—an office worker, family member, foreigner or friend—before the end of this Valentine month.

6

The What, Where and Why of Love

Prior to the late 1300s, Valentine's Day had no connection with romance. In fact, the love celebrated to honor St. Valentine was purely platonic. Today the tables have turned. Greeting cards, flowers, jewelry and chocolates are mostly geared toward stirring up passion, not promoting unadulterated devotion.

The history of poor Valentinus aside, his feast's unintended transition from kindness to craving does raise a significant dilemma: Where is the line between loving and lusting? One key to unlocking this quandary is to explore the mystery of love itself. How? We can examine three queries: What is love? Where is love? Why does love exist at all?

What is love? Without discounting the emotional underpinnings like physical attraction and gratification, in the end, pure love really comes down to a decision. Aquinas' definition is brief and to the point: willing the good of another. When firefighters run into a building to rescue trapped individuals from being burned to death, they are willing the good of another. That is what love is.

Where is love? Lionel Bart's musical adaptation of the Dickens' classic began with a forlorn Oliver Twist looking for love in all the wrong places. However, by the end of the song, the grungy orphan in the title role of *Oliver!* learns that pristine love does not fall from the sky or grow under trees. Rather, true love resides in our ability to bond with another.

Why is love? This, of course, is the most complicated investigation of all. Even the most rigidly atheistic scientists today are compelled to admit that there really is no rational justification for love to have spontaneously appeared on the evolutionary ladder. But it did. The human species could have easily survived and even thrived on biological drives alone. So why do we also place ourselves in harm's way for complete strangers? Why do we find ourselves caring at all? Why do we fall in love? Here we must turn to Augustine's reply: Our hearts are made for Thee, O Lord, and they will not rest until they rest in Thee. We love because we are made in the image and likeness of God, who is love.

HOLY HOMEWORK

We can anonymously send a Valentine's Day card to an organization such as those supporting police officers, firefighters, or veterans, thanking them for the service they provide out of purely human love.

7

The Language
of Love

Traveling abroad? Some studies suggest that we can express our basic needs in any foreign tongue if we know as few as 500 root words along with some fundamental rules of grammar. According to the Guinness Book of Records, the Greeks command the richest verbal communication skills in the world because they have more words than any other language: five million, plus 70 million derivatives. English has only a smidgen over 1,025,000 words! Why? Perhaps our vocabulary is undersized because we use the same word to mean many different things.

All You Need Is Love

For example, in English we use one word, love, in reference to everything from people and pets to ice cream and art. The Greeks begin their exploration of what love means with at least seven different words. We can almost intuit their fine distinctions at first glance. *Éros* (erotic, passionate love), *philía* (brotherly love, as in the city named Philadelphia), *mania* (insane, frenzied, possessive love), *ludus* (avoiding commitment, playful love), *pragma* (logical, making compromises, practical love), *storgê* (slowly developing, stable love), and *agápe* (altruistic, selfless love). This last entry mirrors the definition by St. Thomas Aquinas: willing the good of another, which moves the concept of love away from an emotion and closer to a choice.

Interestingly though, a computer search in English for the definition of the word love yields more than 600 million entries, which implies either a lot of love a lot of repetition, a lot of confusion, or both of those and more. And product marketing campaigns don't make it any easier for us to understand this four-letter word.

From Christmas to Valentines

From December 26 forward through the weeks following, on many store shelves, we begin looking at chocolate-filled treats arranged in red, heart-shaped gift boxes. Like the commercialization of Christmas, poor Valentine's Day has fallen victim to the transfer of heartfelt loving into heart-filled gifting. Vendors have taken financial advantage of flowers, jewelry, greeting cards and candy by turning them into expressions of so-called real love. But real love, as Aquinas declares, is an act of the will. In other words, authentic love is expressed by a decision about how we are going to treat others; by our behavior toward them.

Dead Declarations Versus Living Manifestations

If our hearts simply sat in our chest cavities and did not pump blood we would die. The same is true of our love. Yes, the words and the emotions and the tokens of affection expressed on February 14 are significant symbols. But they are dead if they are void of love in action. After all, what are we really celebrating on Valentine's Day? Hopefully, we are professing true love. What is true love? It is not empty calories, clever words, expensive gems, or even passionate kisses. Love, if it is true, must always, ultimately, manifest itself in behavior. If a spouse says, "I love you" but refuses to empty the dishwasher, the couple experiences an immediate disconnect between a declaration of love and a manifestation of love.

God's Spirited Love

The Bible assures us that our heavenly Father is eager to mercifully forgive our sins and fill us with grace. How so? The prophet Ezekiel reveals this promise to us when God says, "I will remove the heart of stone from your flesh and give you a heart of flesh. I will put my spirit within you..." (Ezekiel 36:26–27).

When God puts his spirit of love inside us, we are receiving the same energy and strength that supported each footstep of Christ in his painful, loving struggle to Calvary. Christ decided to die for us out of love for us. So when we say we truly love others, we are deciding to suffer for their good and give up our lives for them. We may need 500 words to navigate a foreign land but we only need one word to follow the path of Christ. And that one word is love.

HOLY HOMEWORK

There are more than a million words with varying definitions in the English language, but what is our personal definition of one word, love? In a conspicuous location like the top of our computer screen, the bathroom mirror, or the refrigerator door, let's place a sticky note with LOVE written on it. This tag can serve as a daily reminder during the month of February of how we define love and how closely we come to willing the good of another.

HAPPY
Easter

**Father,
enlighten us with the Spirit
of the risen Son.**

Our Lenten Gardens

The Garden of Eden

God created Adam and Eve and placed them in a garden called Eden. The word Eden means God's garden or a place that is fruitful and has plenty of water. We were not only created in God's image and likeness but also formed from the rich ground of God's own garden. Therefore, besides being a ray of light that illuminates the faith of those who feel doubtful and a dash of salt that preserves the hope of those who feel discouraged, we are also a spiritual soil that can germinate seeds of love for those who feel separated and alone. In God's garden, we are a parcel of land for others.

Lent is the perfect opportunity to ask ourselves: How is our patch of Eden growing? What weeding, tilling, and attention is needed in our section of God's good earth so that the seeds of evangelization can take root and flourish?

The Covenantal Garden

Through their disobedience to God's command, as well as our continued disobedience to God's covenant, Adam and Eve abused the beautiful garden God had given them. Instead of basking in innocence, they stripped leaves from the vines to cover their naked bodies. The lie of the fork-tongued serpent, who promised they would become as smart as God, quickly gave way to the truth. They discovered that once separated from the vine, branches and leaves wither away quickly and die. Whenever creatures defy the Creator, the joyful Garden of Eden becomes a sorrowful valley of tears.

The Garden of Gethsemane

Each time we separate ourselves from the true vine we are choosing to stray from living heartily in God's garden and preferring to exist in a self-centered desert of heartbreak. Jesus saw our misguided choices when he himself agonized for us in the Garden of Gethsemane. Through tears of our own making we often cry out this question: "Why, if God is all knowing, and all powerful and all benevolent, is suffering even permitted?" The rhetorically convincing answer, albeit sadly erroneous, is that suffering must exist because of free will. This reply "works" but it is deceiving. In the place of such sophistry we should defer to St. Thomas Aquinas and remember that bad arguments for the sake of the faith bring bad credit upon the faith. Suffering exists so that we can intervene with mercy. Each time we see misery but refuse to pray for the downtrodden, we are refusing to show mercy and we are turning away from God and our neighbor. Each time we see starvation but refuse to fast and feed the hungry, we are refusing to show mercy and turning away from God and our neighbor. Each time we pass a homeless person and refuse to give alms, we are refusing to show mercy and turning away from God and our neighbor. Whenever we avoid an occasion to alleviate suffering we are prolonging hardship and thereby causing suffering. In the end, we are misusing our free will to hurt rather than help. As a substitute for giving praise to God and showing charity to our neighbor, we are turning away from both and preferring sin to virtue.

The Garden of Glory

We humans began life in a garden, and our salvation, our new life, was first made known to us in a garden. The sepulcher, which held the dead body of Jesus, was located in a garden. Three days after the crucifixion and burial, Mary Magdalene was so upset by his empty tomb that she mistook Christ for the gardener. In her joy at finally recognizing him, Magdalene desperately clung to the risen Lord and refused to let go. Christ gently reminded her, and us, that there is still much to be done in the garden of our world before we can ascend to the garden in paradise. Through our faith, our good works and our baptism into Christ's passion, death, resurrection, and ascension, we have the potential to return to Eden. We can become fruitful and multiply the mercy God has shown to us by showing mercy to others. Baptism is God's Holy Spirit of living water bubbling up within us, as Jesus promised the woman at the well, to quench our thirst for righteousness. Our purpose on earth is to transform our hardened hearts into natural hearts longing for that heavenly space which God desires for each of us. How can we bring about this transformation?

Our Lenten Garden

We can prepare for our space in heaven by examining our space on earth. How orderly are we? What does our space look like? Is the space where we live and work very cluttered? Lent is a wonderful time to get organized. To tidy up our home and our workspace, we can begin by examining the state of our hearts and our souls. How readily do we receive God and others? Are the different gardens of our lives strewn with shriveled up leaves that are dying because we have separated ourselves from the true, life-giving vine? Do we ignore the expiration date of canned goods in our cupboards until we are forced to toss this sustenance into the garbage while the shelves of food pantries for the poor become barren? Have we accrued so much furniture and clothing that we need stackable bins to store our excess while the aisles at the St. Vincent de Paul stores fall empty?

Like any seasoned grower, every Christian knows there are plagues of pests threatening to prevent the growth of our attempts to be kind and compassionate. Temptations to prolong the disobedience of our progenitors towards God abound. Lent is a time to rid our gardens—our homes, our work spaces, our hearts and our souls—of those allures that exclude God and shun others. The cultivating tools we need are easily available. They are prayer, fasting, and almsgiving. All we have to do is put them into practice. Then our Garden of Gethsemane will become a renewed Garden of Eden. Our garden of Covenant will become a garden of Glory toward God and a welcoming haven for all.

HOLY HOMEWORK

For the duration of Lent, let's place a symbol of our interior garden, like a flower, in our kitchen and at our workspace. Each morning when we see this reminder we can ask ourselves: What can I do today to declutter my house, my heart, and my soul so that all of my gardens are properly prepared to receive my struggling neighbor and my risen Lord this Easter?

Remembering
and Forgetting

What We Long to Forget

When I was in my late twenties, a wiser and much older priest told me that one of God's greatest gifts to humans was our ability to forget. Until that moment, I had only heard senior citizens complain about poor recollection. They would lament about how their memory wasn't what it used to be. How quick their responses were when they were younger but, now that they were older, how hard they had to concentrate just to recall the simplest thing. Yet here was an ancient, saintly cleric extolling the virtue of forgetfulness. He never offered an example at the time but we all have experiences we would prefer to dismiss than retain. Some of the childhood trials we would gladly put to sleep can be the very thoughts that keep us awake at night, wishing they had never happened. A dressing down from a grammar school teacher, a stern rebuke from the phys ed coach, a scurrilous name-calling tag from the classroom bully—what we wouldn't give to lay these scars to rest and forget where we buried them.

What We Long to Remember

"Please remember" were the two words that stayed with me long after I left their small apartment. Do you know the worst time of the week to call on a priest? Sunday afternoon. Our Saturday morning Mass can be followed by a 10 AM funeral, followed by a mid-afternoon wedding, followed by one or two anticipated Sunday Masses with at least two more subsequent liturgies the next morning plus baptisms at 1 PM. Trust me, you do not want to phone the rectory at 3 o'clock in the afternoon on the Lord's Day of rest to ask for a favor.

But that's when he called me. John F. Junior from the retirement complex on the other side of town. Could I bring holy Communion to him and the anointing of the sick to his wife? I said yes and dragged myself to the tabernacle to retrieve a consecrated host for my pyx. With the oil of the infirmed, a reversible purple and white stole and the ritual book in my pocket, I prayed for strength and that the traffic would be light. It wasn't. Nor was I thrilled about this duty. Why didn't God arrange an easier appointment for me at a more convenient hour during the week?

Mr. J. F. Jr., a surprisingly spry ninety-two-year-old gent, greeted me warmly at the entrance to their tiny abode. Through an archway, I spied his white-haired wife, whom I guessed to be around the same age, sitting in a rocking chair staring off into space. John whispered that he could receive the Eucharist but his wife could not. She was suffering from the advanced stages of Alzheimer's and might not remember she was supposed to swallow the host. As he led me closer to her rocker she glanced up at me for a split second, blinked twice and then went back to staring at the wall. John turned to me with excitement. "Did you see that, Father?" he asked. "Did you see her reaction to you?" Honestly, to me her glance was trivial but not to him. He wondered if my black suit or white Roman collar had caused her response. He hoped that my entrance or my attire had somehow jogged her memory with an association from the past. Something. Anything.

Next I witnessed the reason God dragged me away from my afternoon melancholy to this tender love scene which I shall never forget. John turned to his wife and increased his volume with, "Look who is here, Minnie. Father is going to bless you. Wasn't that nice of him to come and see you?" No response. Then he proceeded to kneel down in front of the lifelong spouse whom he was losing on a daily basis. He gently grasped her right hand in his left and lifted it to her forehead. He began making the sign of the cross with both their fingers intertwined, repeating the words they had exchanged long ago on their wedding day, "In the name of the Father...do you remember, Minnie," he interjected into the Trinitarian formula, "...and of the Son...please remember, Minnie, please. Please remember one more time...And of the Holy Spirit..." his voice giving way to tear drops falling onto her lap.

Do this in Memory of Me
On the first Holy Thursday, Jesus ate the Passover Meal with his apostles. As it turned out this was also his Last Supper. He knew he would be leaving them the next day. Perhaps he felt torn. Perhaps he was eager to return to his Father but at the same time wanting to stay. Even kneeling down in front of them and washing their feet wasn't enough to teach them about true leadership. So how could he help them remember? Simple. By not leaving at all. He would change the substance of bread and

wine into his own Body and Blood and assure them that each time they did this, he would be present. No need to work to remember. No chance to ever forget. I am here. Do this and remember yourself with Me. Each year on Holy Thursday, we recall what many people easily forget: that, in the end, Christ loved us so much he could not leave us.

HOLY HOMEWORK

Let's make time this month to visit folks at a local nursing home and leave a spray of flowers or a small plant at the nurses' station. Let's assure the staff that they and their residents will be remembered in our prayers in a special way this Holy Thursday.

Mad as Hell
at Easter

Where in the Sam Hill did we learn to coin a phrase in English? Once in a blue moon we should wet our whistle about the etymology of our colloquialisms by introducing an ice breaker that would keep us from throwing in the towel or giving up the ghost on this subject. And that was just the first seven that came to mind.

My mother rarely got upset. But when she did she used the expression, "I'm mad as hell." Since she never added the trailer "and I'm not going to take this anymore," I have to assume that this particular idiom predated *Network*, the 1976 movie where that saying was prominent.

Exactly how far back does the idea "mad as hell" go, and who was the first to introduce it? I believe we can trace its origins to a doctor of the Church, St. John Chrysostom, around the year 400, in his famous Easter sermon. But why did hell get so mad? Because when Christ died and descended into its midst, hell could not hold onto his body. Christ rose again and this put all hell in an uproar—hence the notion: mad as hell. St. John writes:

Hell was in an uproar because it was done away with.
It was in an uproar because it was mocked.
It was in an uproar, for it was destroyed.
It was in an uproar, for it was annihilated.
It was in an uproar, for it was now made captive.
Hell took a body, and discovered God.
It took earth, and encountered heaven.
It took what it saw, and was overcome by what it did not see.

Some say that people are getting madder these days due to the economy, advertising pressures to buy more, labor pressures to do more, social pressures to be more successful and to look more beautiful and so on. Others suggest that we are not angrier nowadays but we do feel freer to express antisocial feelings that we used to keep secret. Have we become as mad as hell?

What happens when Catholics do something nice for other people, even something as simple as allowing them to cut in front of us in traffic or step ahead of us at the checkout counter? Every time we do a good deed for someone else, we are celebrating the risen joy of Easter, our freedom from sin and our freedom to choose to do good for others. And we are also making hell very angry.

HOLY HOMEWORK

Each day during the Easter season, let's perform an act of kindness for someone. This will get hell mad. Make no mistake about it!

We Love Our
Easter Potholes

The severe winter leaves its imprint on New York City pavement in the form of potholes; lots of them. Dings, dents, and damages take a back seat for those drivers who must regularly replace a steering rod due to these asphalt chasms. It's enough to make people take public transportation, unless they earn a living by operating one of the city's 13,000 taxis or more than 60,000 other for-hire vehicles.

Bear in mind the Empire State is not number one in the nation when it comes to these macadam cavities. Imagine what it must be like to maneuver a motor vehicle around one of the five states that rank ahead of us when it comes to rim-eating road craters. So, what's a Catholic cabbie to do? Offer it up? That's certainly one option. But there's an alternate approach, which is just as Christian and more in keeping with the reason for this resurrection season.

Since winter patches are temporary, the more permanent pothole fixes have to wait until springtime. So instead of getting upset, we can shift to a more spiritual solution for enduring these bumps in the road. And this solution fits rather nicely with the coming of Easter, particularly the paschal Triduum, which begins with the Last Supper on Holy Thursday and concludes with Evening Prayer on Easter Sunday. The fractures in the freeway on our way to work can actually conjure up some very valuable meditations, if we let them.

Holy Thursday, Men at Work

Ever pass by one man shoveling while two others are leaning? Instead of lamenting the apparent lack of bang for tax bucks, we can offer a genuine prayer for the flagmen and crew workers. If we assume this kinder attitude toward others, we mirror the humble, kneeling position that Christ took when he washed his disciples' feet. Plus, it affords us time to ask: How often are we quick to judge people instead of giving them the benefit of the doubt?

Good Friday, No Easy Path to Calvary

GPS trackers may be able to suggest a less congested route, but so far they haven't been able to give us a heads-up on which highways are filled with fissures. And until they do, we will have to swerve to avoid bumping into a street gap. But this veering action can also remind us to ask: How seriously are we steering clear of the temptation to sin? The daily crosses we must bear are rarely lightweight and the passage to our personal Calvary is neither paved nor smooth.

Holy Saturday, the Unmovable Mausoleum

Ironically, instead of rejoicing when the tar trucks are on the scene, we get frustrated because they force us to merge into fewer lanes or, even worse, bring traffic to a screeching halt. Now we're no longer hitting holes at fifty-five or more miles per hour because we're standing dead still. This is the moment to breathe, relax, and use this downtime to meditate on death, as the saints did. Holy Saturday is tomb day. What legacy will we leave behind for the benefit of others when we're buried beneath a cold stone marker?

On Easter, Commuters Are Up to Speed

Alleluia, eventually the roads get repaired and traffic moves along nicely. Easter is akin to driving on a newly opened, free-of-charge expressway. No bumps, no clefts, no tolls to pay. Just clear sailing and sunny skies ahead for as far as the eye can see. This is a driver's taste of heaven. Do we remember to thank God when our lives are well-tuned and running fine?

HOLY HOMEWORK

Affix a small sign to the dashboard that reads: "We Love Our Easter Potholes." When a passenger asks why, explain: "These bumps force us to slow down in this hectic, stressful world. These holes give us time to pause and meditate on the more important aspects of life." Keep this reminder note on display until the end of summer, when all of the potholes will be gone, hopefully.

Happy Mother's Day

Mary, virgin and mother,
perpetually help all women to
bring Christ into the world.

12

Capacity
12,045
Cubic Inches

The typical metal shopping cart that we push up and down the aisles at the grocery store is designed to hold an average of 12,045 cubic inches of foodstuffs. But anyone who lives in New York City knows these glossy wagons can hold much more. Stand on the corner of almost any intersection and in no time at all you'll hear one of these squeaking cages meandering down the street, overloaded beyond its stated volume with anything and everything except the produce it was intended to carry.

Obscuring the insignia that identifies the establishment where the carriage belongs and hiding the rusted plate that warns "Do Not Remove From Store" is a collection of discarded rubbish: garbage to us all; all the world to the beggar barely visible behind the heaps of trash, trinkets and tattered clothing piled to teetering heights.

Despite their ubiquity, it's rare that any of us actually *meets* one of these street people. But once upon a time, a priest confrere and I did. We discovered later that her name was Jeannie. Eighteen months after our solitary encounter, we learned that Jeannie had a daughter named Margaret. But like most of us, her daughter preferred to look the other way. She was ashamed to admit that her mother was homeless. She had forgotten that underneath the knotted gray hair and the layers of shabby overcoats was a woman who loved her. But even though this daughter long ago disowned her mother, the opposite was not true. Jeannie never forgot Margaret.

One bone-chilling wintry night, Jeannie approached the rear entrance to our rectory. If we had not been in the kitchen at that exact moment, we would never have heard her soft rapping on our window. Generally we don't open the door to strangers. It simply isn't done in the city. But this intrusion was so unexpectedly delicate, the tapping sounded more like an embarrassed apology even before we saw the weary face and threadbare glove behind the knock. Her other hand, uncovered and riddled with arthritis, clutched two ends of a fraying head scarf gathered beneath her chin.

We never asked what she wanted. Everyone knows what these folks often want: some kind of handout. A sandwich and a soda or a few bucks will usually send them away quickly. Of course there's always the danger that if you give money, they'll keep coming back for more. We were tempted to refer Jeannie to a city agency for the indigent, but she never gave us that chance.

As soon as we opened the door, she began rummaging through her lopsided pushcart to retrieve a buried treasure. She handed us a large coffee can stuffed with grimy dollar bills and a note printed in old-people's handwriting:

"For my Margie. I sorry I never make you a proud of me. Luv momie."

Beneath the message was her daughter's phone number. But by the time we were able to locate her, the destitute donor had vanished. We don't know what became of her. Perhaps she died from frostbite that winter, shivering under a cardboard box. Maybe she wanders the avenues of the city to this day, filling 12,045 cubic inches of cart with refuse to exchange for pennies, nickels, and dimes for her child. But wherever you are, Jeannie, Margaret sends her love.

HOLY HOMEWORK

Sometime during this month of May, instead of crossing the street to avoid a bag lady, extend a gesture of Christian compassion toward her in appreciation for the maternal care we have received.

Happy Mother's Day to all our moms.

From Mother
to Child

Researcher, author, and mother of two sons, Christine Peet writes:
One of the most difficult things for mothers and fathers is worrying about keeping their children safe. Whether it is protection from the neighborhood bully, or to the extreme, literally keeping them alive, we worry (Association for Research on Mothering, York University, Toronto).

The Virgin Mary failed miserably as a mother on both these counts. From the governors of the Roman community to the high priests of the Jewish community, Christ was continually harassed by bullies wherever he went. Nor could Mary keep Jesus alive. She could weep for him during his false trial with its cruel beatings and inhumane tortures. She could rail against the irony of a sign hung above his head calling him a king in three languages as he was nailed to a throne of humiliating crucifixion. She could wrap his cold and lifeless body in strips of swathing clothes to bury him quickly in a crib of stone. But none of her worrying or weeping or wrapping could keep him safe or keep him alive.

He was too much like her. She had taught him too well. He was just as obedient in doing God's will as she had been.

The greatest tribute a child can pay to his or her parents is this innate imitation of who their parents are and what they stand for. This is an imitation because it is learned from them, handed down from them. This is an innate virtue because it is born from them, a piece of them.

Obedience was part of the fabric of his mother, Mary, which Jesus inherited and learned well. From the age of sixteen, when God sent Gabriel to ask her for a favor, she responded obediently with one word, yes. Christmas celebrates obedience, birth over waiting. Easter celebrates obedience, life over death. This same obedience is mirrored in the sacraments, religious vows, and after every prayer we offer up to God. I do. I am here. Amen. So may it be.

Husbands and wives exchange their obedient fidelity to one another in the sacrament of marriage. Do you promise to be faithful? I do. The bishop calls the clergy candidate to orders. He answers, I am present, I am here, send me where you need me and I will go, I will obey. The first meaning of the word *amen* is a form of obedience: so be it. In other words, we make this prayer with the hope of a certain outcome, but we understand and agree that the final outcome may be different. And if that different outcome is what God wants, then that's OK with us.

HOLY HOMEWORK

Write down three virtues that come to mind when you think about your mother. Slip this paper into an envelope and write the word AMEN across the seal. Carry the envelope with you for the next 30 days and each time you become aware of it, offer a prayer of thanksgiving for mom and ask yourself if obedience is valued nowadays. Happy Mother's Day.

A Sainted Pope's Virtues for American Motherhood

He was only ten years into his papacy of more than twenty-six years when St. John Paul II published his encyclical on the *Dignity of Women*. In this letter he repeated the word *motherhood* 60 times and the word *mother* 122 times. Although he highlighted many maternal virtues throughout the document, these three are particularly reflective of our American celebration of Mother's Day: Trusting Cooperation, Self-sacrificing Service and Life-giving Unity.

Trusting Cooperation

Many people associate the annunciation event with Mary's attitude of humility and obedience. After all it was her let-it-be-done-to-me *fiat* that led to her being given the title "New Eve," suggesting a far more compliant maidservant of the Lord. But St. John Paul reminds us that the underlying quality, which brings Mary's consent into focus, is less about deference or acquiescence and more about the virtue of trust. In the end she said yes to the Archangel Gabriel because she trusted he was telling her the truth. In this third millennium of doubt and uncertainty it is our mothers who wisely encourage us to be astutely trusting of others and to be transparently trustworthy ourselves.

Self-sacrificing Service

Mary's trust not only brought her into divine motherhood through the Holy Spirit but also into the mission of the Christ Child she bore. John Paul indicates she carried in her body the Savior of the world and she carried in her heart his mission of self-sacrificing service toward others. As he grew in wisdom and grace at their humble Nazareth home, we can be confident that the self-sacrificing service of Jesus' mother helped him to prepare for his mission on earth. When he was an infant, how often did Mary wash Jesus' feet? Later he would teach his disciples how to become true leaders by washing their feet. When he was young, how often did Mary doctor his scrapes and bruises? Later he would authenticate his identity by healing the sick and restoring to health those who were sickened by sin. When he was a man, how often did a sword pierce Mary's heart as she followed him all the way to Calvary? Later he would shed blood and water by the sword of a soldier as he brought to completion his Father's covenant of love for all people. Our mothers continue to model self-sacrificing service so we can extend this Christian mission toward others.

Life-giving Unity

Mothers give life to people. And because we are human, we are never born into isolation. Rather we are born to live in solidarity and in harmony with others. This, according to St. John Paul, is the true meaning of our being made *in the image and likeness of God.* Our mothers encourage us to get along with others. Why? So that when our smile reflects the reality of our kinship with our neighbor, our face also reflects the image of our likeness to God. Our physical attributes mirror the features of the woman who gave us life, our mother. Whenever we peer deeply into Mom's eyes, we realize we are, in so many ways, a reflection of her life. And if we follow her example by choosing to live in genuine connection with other people, we will breathe a life-giving spirit of unity into all our relationships. Then, when we look into other people's eyes, we will see a reflection of the image and likeness of God.

HOLY HOMEWORK

During the month of May let's keep a tiny mirror at our desk or in our pocket. Let's look into this mirror at least once a day and remember two things: to offer a prayer of thanksgiving for our mothers in whose temporal image we were born, and to offer a prayer of thanksgiving to God our Creator in whose eternal image we were made.

St. John Paul the Great, pray for us.

15

Mothers:
Modern-Day Heroes
or Merely Moms?

A neighbor runs into a burning house and saves a child from certain death. The 6 o'clock news labels him Superman, but he replies that he was only doing what needed to be done. Apparently, he is a hero in everyone's mind except his own.

What about mothers? Are they modern-day heroes or merely being moms?

Last month I asked my college students to name one person in the world who is a great hero. I speculated that some would list highly visible Change Agents who are trying to impact international social issues like pollution, politics and the global economy. I suspected that other responses would run the gamut from cartoon action figures to Hollywood rock stars. But I'm happy to report that my conjectures were wrong and their answers surprised me.

Topping the chart by a landslide was their mom, with their dad following closely behind and grandparents bringing up a distant third. The remainder of the list included cousins, friends, and popular celebrities, but these only garnered 1 or 2 percentage points at best.

Obviously, the phenomenal perseverance and selfless dedication of some single moms who are working full time, maintaining a household, raising a family and putting at least one child through college does not go unnoticed in the eyes of today's young adults. But if we asked these women if they considered themselves heroes, most would smile and say they were merely being moms. They are mothers who are "loving their children into adulthood" with strength that would astonish Iron Man and patience that would impress Saint Teresa of Calcutta.

"My mom raised me by herself, clothed me, fed me, instilled good morals in me and she still pays the bulk of my tuition by working double shifts and taking care of my younger sister at home," writes one young woman of nineteen. "Of course she is my hero. Who else could hold a candle to what she's done for me?"

"I don't thank her enough, I know that," admits a lanky fellow who sits in the back of the classroom. "My mom doesn't speak English very well, but she works harder and puts in longer hours than any man I know. In middle school my pants never seemed to fit right because I was growing so fast. Other kids would laugh because my cuffs rose above my ankles.

But I didn't care. My mom couldn't afford the latest styles so I never said anything. I knew she'd be hurt if I did. My silence was the only gift of thanks I could give her back then. Someday I will be successful. Then I will pay her back so she can relax and live the better life that she deserves. She's more than my hero. I think of her as my 'wonder mom' because I wonder how she keeps going without getting tired."

HOLY HOMEWORK

This Mother's Day, let's send a note of gratitude from our hearts and offer a special prayer for the unsung woman in our lives who would never label herself a modern-day hero, because in her heart she's just merely being a mom.

16

Mother of Mercy

In this month of May as we celebrate Mother's Day, is there any better time to reflect upon Mary who is not only a mother but also a mother of mercy? Let's begin with an analysis of her merciful role as delineated in an ancient prayer invoking her help, then let's add the thoughts of a great doctor of the Church, St. Alphonsus Mary Liguori, and let's conclude with some of the most cherished attributes of motherhood, which are being heralded today.

Hail Holy Queen

According to its popular English translation, the Hail Holy Queen prayer, known in Latin as the *Salve Regina*, starts off with no less than seven different salutations. Surprisingly, not one of these seven greetings addresses Mary by her given name. Instead we greet her as a holy woman, a woman of royalty, a mother and a person who is merciful, life-giving, sweet and in whom we place our hope.

Although this is a very brief prayer, the association of Mary with mercy occurs three separate times. At the start of the prayer, we hail her as the Mother of Mercy. Later on, we implore her to look at us through eyes filled with mercy. Finally, at the end of the prayer, we praise her as a woman of clemency, which is simply another word for mercy.

We may mistakenly believe that the intent of this prayer is to remind Mary to help us because she is the embodiment of all these virtues, especially mercy. But this is not true. On the contrary, the intent of this prayer is to remind ourselves that we should never despair. No matter how far we have drifted away from her Son, we can be confident that Mary will intercede on our behalf. In this way, she is our hope that God will listen to her intervention and temper the justice we deserve with generously underserved mercy instead.

St. Alphonsus Mary (1696–1787)

Of the eight names given to him at his baptism: Alphonsus, Mary, Anthony, John, Cosmas, Damian, Michael, and Gaspard, we might easily conclude that this great moral theologian cherished the patronage of Mary most. He certainly placed salvific hope in her intervention for mercy. Published in 1750, Alphonsus devoted the entire first chapter of his classic work *The Glories of Mary* to explaining her merciful love for us. For example, using common, pastoral metaphors, he says Mary presents us with milk and wool. "The milk of mercy inspires us with confidence and the wool of protection shields us from any punishment we justly deserve for our sins." Here again we see how confidence in being treated with mercy prevents us from falling into despair. To further quell any anxieties we might have, Alphonsus adds another dimension of mercy, namely protection against the pain of being punished. Both images remain apropos today. Milk is still a strengthening nutrient and wool is still a protection against the sting of winter.

Modern Attributes of Motherhood

Which are the most cherished characteristics associated with motherhood today? Mom embodies far too many virtues to list here. But these twenty-five surface regularly during internet searches: life-giving, caring, boundary-setter, consistent, discipliner, trustworthy, teaches, models, patient, prayerful, selfless, supportive, protective, worries, hardworking, listens, perceptive, consoles, applauds, merciful, forgiving, affectionate, joyful, loving and lovable. These traits tend to be more palatable when we transpose them from taxonomy to narrative like so:

The word *mother* means life-giving because she is the woman who not only gave us life but also points us toward the path which keeps us fully alive. From birth she cared enough to set clear boundaries for us and she was consistent in meting out discipline when we dared to cross the line. At every stage of our life she was the one person who was always trustworthy because she always trusted in God. She was our first teacher, a model of patience, who also taught us to pray. Her selfless, unconditional support protected us from any and all who would harm us. And even after we left the nest she continued to worry about us and to pray for our well-being. As hardworking as she was and continues to be, she always takes time to listen to us. Her keen perception anticipates our need for consolation when we fail and our expectation of applause when we succeed. She mercifully forgives and forgets the times we forget and neglect her. Her affection, joy and love for us make her the lovable gift of our world. As the poet Robert Browning said so well, all love begins and ends in motherhood.

HOLY HOMEWORK

Let's post this simple reminder in our work area: When was the last time I contacted or offered a prayer for Mom?

Happy FATHER'S DaY

Saint Joseph,
provider and protector,
strengthen all men to love faithfully
those in their care.

Why Fathers Pray

A most amazing June in my life occurred during my first summer vacation home from the seminary. This was also the first summer that my brother, nine years my junior, was home from the Air Force. On our first Saturday night together, Mom asked us which Mass we were going to attend the next morning. My brother replied that he was NOT going to church with us at all. And, to my parents' dismay, he added that he had not been to church since he moved out of the house.

Crowded around the small kitchen table, the three of them started hashing out the pros and cons of regular church attendance. Actually, the debate was mostly between my mother and my brother. Dad wasn't clever with words. He usually listened and nodded a lot in agreement with whatever my mom said. But this time he was strangely still. I sat at a safe distance preferring the role of silent supporter to religious consultant.

After hours of philosophical debate and with my stubborn sibling showing no change of heart, my exasperated mother summoned me to the table to explain the theological reasons why the Catholic Church insisted that we attend Mass every week. I recall waxing eloquently about justice and how we humans owed God at least one hour of worship in return for all the graces we received. God was the creator. We were the creatures. The commandments were clear. We were obligated to worship God alone and to keep holy the Lord's day. The Church's interpretation of those directives was that we should pray as a community once a week, at the minimum. And that, in a nutshell, was why we went to church.

Still, my brother was unmoved. Then, much to my surprise, my mother's shock, and my brother's utter disbelief, my father spoke up. He announced that obligation was not the reason he showed up at church each week. When my brother asked him why he went, dad said, "I go to pray for you. I can't watch over you like I did when you were little. I can't protect you anymore or try to teach you right from wrong. So, I rely on God. I go to church and pray that God will guide you through the tough times."

Then came Sunday. My dad was up bright and early to attend the very first service of the day which he had always done for as long as I could remember. Mom and I were ready, of course. But we also witnessed a minor miracle that morning. My brother, who was unaware that 6 o'clock came twice a day, was awake and dressed at the crack of dawn. The four of us went to church together without comment, hassle, coaxing or complaint and my brother hasn't missed a Sunday since. Apparently intellectual arguments with young people about church attendance fall by the wayside when they discover simply, why fathers pray.

Happy Father's Day!

HOLY HOMEWORK

Let's locate a favorite snapshot of our father and crop a copy of it to a size that fits easily in our wallet or change purse. We can paperclip this picture to the credit card or currency we use most often. For the next month, each time we make a transaction and see dad's face, let's offer a silent prayer of thanks to honor the man who offered more silent prayers for us than we may ever know.

18

Beyond the
Little-League Dad

A nervous thirty-something father asked to speak with me recently. He said he was having doubts about whether or not he was doing a good enough job at being a dad. Instead of exploring what precipitated his doubts I took a different approach.

"Lee," I asked him, "What's your strongest, positive experience of fatherhood?" He thought for a moment and replied, "I'm not sure if this is the best example but what comes to mind is a particular Little League game I took my youngest son to a few years ago."

"Tell me what happened," I urged. He began by saying, "I remember the day was overcast and humid, very humid. In fact, I was hoping it would rain to cool things off a bit. Alvin asked me if his team would automatically lose the game if it rained. He hadn't been playing well all season. I was afraid he might be looking for an excuse to leave, so I reminded him about the difference between forfeiting a game because of a no-show and rescheduling it due to bad weather. I told him all he had to do was play his best and try not to be distracted by anything around him. I wanted him to learn values like good sportsmanship, team spirit, being responsible, and not looking for an easy way out or running away from commitments. He was only nine. Maybe I was expecting too much. I don't know."

"Sounds to me like you were trying to give your son some good advice. Does that fit?" I asked. "Yeah, I guess so," he said with a shrug. "Anyway, there was a long delay midway through the game. The rain came down in buckets but didn't cool off the temperature much. The infield got soggy and his team lost. But it's what happened after the game that I'll never forget."

"And what was that?" I asked. Lee replied, "I had parked our van on the grass at the far end of the field and a visitor I'd never seen before had parked about three car lengths in front of me. He was slightly older than the other parents and he had to use a wheelchair. After the heavy rain, he must have struggled a lot get back to his vehicle because I remember seeing two deep ruts in the ground that were obviously the tracks left behind by his wheelchair. As Alvin and I walked by his car, I noticed that he had managed to fold his chair into the back seat OK. But somehow, as he was trying to maneuver himself into the front seat, his feet got crossed and twisted together. So, there he was, struggling to get his own two feet apart but he couldn't. They were all tangled up and dangling outside his car door."

"What did you do?" I asked. "What could I do?" Lee shrugged. "I gave Alvin my keys and told him to wait for me in the van while I helped this man out. The poor guy looked so embarrassed when I approached him and I felt pretty awkward myself because I had never knelt down in the mud before to untangle someone else's feet for them. He was so grateful. He even offered me some money afterward, but I wouldn't take anything. I couldn't."

"And then what happened?" I asked. Lee paused for a long time and swallowed hard. I could see he was reliving the experience as his eyes filled up and he stared down into the palms of his hands, jamming his fingers together, twisting them, and then pulling them apart. "I got into the van and I started to cry," he admitted. "I kept telling myself I shouldn't be crying in front of my boy but I couldn't help it."

I waited until Lee regained his composure to ask, "And what are your tears about right now? Do you know?" I was surprised at how quickly he nodded his head.

"Yes," he whispered. "I think I know exactly what my tears are about: that I'm grateful for my own health; that I'm a good person and a strong man but also very caring; and that my son was there to see all that in me. At least I hope he thinks about me that way."

To all the dads who ever doubted their paternal advice, to all the dads who have chauffeured kids to games so they could learn the deeper values of life, and to all the dads who have knelt in the muddy waters of trying to untangle other peoples' problems or stood up tall with watery eyes full of compassion:

Happy Father's Day.

HOLY HOMEWORK

Let's tie two pieces of string together by making four knots in them and placing them in the center of the kitchen counter. Then once each week, for the next four weeks, untie one of those knots while offering a prayer of strength for fathers and mothers and all those who strive to help others untangle the gnarls in their lives.

19

Sit Down, Daddy

Not long ago, I was in my doctor's lobby reading a wrinkled, out-of-date issue of a trendy magazine. I was hoping my annual physical wouldn't take up too much more of my day but sometimes the shortest office visits can stretch into hours. So, I decided to distract myself with a brainteaser. One of the journal articles purported to contain the 100 most popular people from the past. I thought it might be fun to see if I could list who they were before reading their names.

I became so focused on the guessing game that I hardly noticed when two men walked through the door at the other end of the waiting room. The older of the two, a teetering gent, shuffled slowly up to the receptionist's window and handed one of the nurses a sheet of paper. She thanked him and he struggled back toward his junior companion who was rifling through a light-blue carryall tote resembling an oversized diaper bag.

"Dad, sit down." The graying son didn't look up from his rummaging. He simply waited a few seconds as if he knew he would be ignored and repeated a tad louder, with a twist, "Sit down, Daddy." The irony of his follow-up vocabulary caught my ear and amused me a bit—a command that would tame a feral child mixed with a term of endearment found on the lips of any two-year-old toddler.

The elder disregarded both instructions. Instead of sitting he began clawing at his overcoat. After what must have seemed like an eternity of wrestling, he finally asked the younger man for help. The dutiful son put the diaper sack aside and rescued his father from his battle with the heavy sleeves. Then he aired his request once more. "Dad, sit down." Another ten-second pause. "Sit down, Daddy." And again, the senior remained standing.

Less than a minute later, their dialogue resumed. Grown-older Daddy, "Do you have that piece of paper for the nurse?" Grown-up Sonny: "You gave it to the receptionist when we came in." Daddy: "I did?" Sonny: "Yes, you did."

The senior made his way back to the sliding window, while the son repeated his respectful lament, this time with his eyes closed and a slight change up: "Sit down, Dad. Daddy, sit down, please."

His father never sat down. He tapped on the glass pane and continued to interrupt the busy women on the inaccessible side of the partition. A different face appeared.

New Nurse, "May I help you?" Daddy, "Do you have the paper I gave you?" New Nurse, "You didn't give me anything, sir. Maybe you gave it to the other nurse." Sonny (from the far end of the room), "Please just tell him you have it or he'll keep asking and drive you all crazy." New Nurse (ignoring the sage advice), "I wasn't the person you gave it to, sir."

The son shook his head in disbelief and repeated his dirge in the same level calm: "Dad, take a seat please. Sit down, Daddy."

"She says I never gave it to her."

"You gave it to the other receptionist when we came in."

"I did?"

"Yes, you did, so now you can come over here and have a seat."

Needless to say, Daddy continued to stand. For the next 15 minutes, he inched around the perimeter of the room. Sometimes he would stop to ask the same question about the initial paperwork. Other times he asked a new query, one more central to their sojourn.

Daddy (annoyed and frustrated), "What are we doing here?" Sonny (not sounding exasperated in the least), "We're at the doctor's office. They said you need to have more blood work done. How about a sit down, Daddy? These chairs are really comfortable. Wanna try one?"

I was amazed that the son never once sounded stern, lost his cool, or talked down to his father in some condescending way. Maybe he was hesitant to scold his dad in public. Maybe he had learned that changing the tone of his voice didn't change the outcome of his dad's behavior. Or maybe he was just raised to be respectful of his elders. Whatever the motivation, he struck me as having the patience of a saint. I imagined that this snapshot from their lives together was just a single frame from the continuous movie of a day spent with Sonny watching Daddy, tirelessly responding to his tiring questions, but resolved never to let him out of his sight, even for a moment.

Perhaps the son was religious and inspired to gentleness by faith. Or maybe he was simply resigned to the fact that his father's condition wasn't going to improve and he wanted their time together to be peaceful. Or maybe he saw deeply into the future and hoped that one day his own son would be spared such a fate or at least be as calm and understanding with him as he was trying to be with his father.

By the time the nurse escorted me into the examining room, I had finished playing the 100 most popular name game. Even though I identified several of them, I knew this caretaker son wouldn't be among them. I thought to myself, he most certainly should be!

HOLY HOMEWORK

Let's contact or pray for Dad today, depending on whether he's living or deceased. We can wish him a happy Father's Day, and if proximity permits, let's sit down with Daddy and be gentle with him...while we can.

20

Fathers and Children, Lettuce and Bargains

My father loved lettuce. For him, a meal was incomplete if it didn't include a huge, leafy green salad. I was never a fan of celery, radishes, or endive. He could have my share at any luncheon spread and twice at supper.

My father loved bargains. Every Saturday he scoured the flea markets of our Florida community for a hidden financial find. And haggling for an even lower price was his particular delight. I loathe shopping. When I need something, I take one look at the price tag and reach for my wallet.

Can opposite attitudes toward lettuce and bargains signal a substantial difference between fathers and their offspring? Despite our adolescent years of longing to be independent of or even opposite from our progenitors, when all is said and done, do we end up growing into carbon copies of the genetic code we inherited at conception?

Last week my return flight to JFK was hopelessly delayed at the Washington Dulles airport. In such an instance my father would say complaining doesn't help and that people should turn negatives into positives. I, however, searched around for a customer service counter so I could lodge a formal grievance. Oddly enough, such a booth was there, but no one was manning it. Typical.

As I checked the monitor for the next projected delay to my itinerary and continued to stress out in ways that my dad would deem silly and counterproductive, I began to wonder if the personality links between fathers and their descendants were so fragile that they disappear within a single generation. Then I saw the strangest thing: a middle-aged gent walking gingerly along while typing a text message into his mobile phone. Judging from his facial features, he could easily have passed for the patriarch of a family of an 18-year-old student in my communications class named Alex. Not only did their physical resemblance match but also their behavioral penchant for electronic wizardry. Alex continually had his head buried in his Android, two thumbs whizzing wildly in a blur over the keypad. Perhaps the "gadgeteer" doesn't fall far from the geek's tree after all.

The long, bending concourse at this airport would beckon my father to take a leisurely stroll. He loved exercise, especially walking. I looked around for the closest chair. Luckily one was tucked under a nearby table beneath a Starbucks sign. I decided I should eat something.

Just as I approached the display case and turned up my nose at their leftover sandwiches, the cashier was placing a brand-new container of crisp Caesar Salad on the top shelf. I pointed and asked how much. For $6.27 with soft drink and chips included, how could I say no? I tugged a few napkins out of the dispenser, plopped down at the empty table, and offered a quick prayer that my dad would intercede for patience on my behalf. Then I took a deep breath and promised I would spend the rest of this trip turning negatives into positives just as he would have done. As I peered into the plastic bowl, it suddenly dawned on me that I had selected a plate of lettuce for my meal and at quite the bargain price. Then, for a fleeting moment, it was as though Daddy was sitting across from me, smiling broadly, and dipping a celery stalk into his favorite mixture of olive oil and pepper.

The Bible says we are all made in the image and likeness of God, our Father. How often do we mirror his behavior and his love?

HOLY HOMEWORK

Select one or two characteristic virtues of our earthly father, or our heavenly Father, and imitate these traits for one whole day in their honor.

And a blessed Father's Day to all our dads.

HOLINESS
& Mercy

Lord, help us tune out noisy
distractions so we can hear
you clearly and listen to one
another deeply.

OMG,
Turn Off
That Phone!

When we were growing up, our family could not afford a private phone. We had to share a party line with three other families. And since all phone bells sounded alike, each residence had its own assigned ring sequence. For example, if the call was for our house, the phone would sound out two short pulses followed by one long ring. If the call was for one of the other three families on our party line, then the signal would be different, perhaps one long ring, or two short rings, or some other combination of these bell pulses.

Sharing a party line also meant that, prior to placing an outgoing call, we needed to pick up the receiver and listen before dialing. If there was a conversation going on, we had to hang up and make the call later when the line was free. For the paranoid, the curious and the neighborhood busybodies who had nothing better to do, eavesdropping on the conversations of others was an easy, unscrupulous pastime.

Eavesdropping notwithstanding, I asked the forty college students I'm teaching this semester to observe a public conversation between two other students on campus and to report back about how effective or ineffective their listening skills were. Not surprisingly, most examples of poor communication involved one person punching text messages into a mobile phone while pretending to be listening to what the other person was saying.

Is anyone surprised by this? Remember when our parents told us to be mindful of others? Mind full! What is our mind filled with these days when we're talking with someone else? Effective listening means paying attention to the other person. Only when our mind is full of nothing else but what the other person is saying are we truly being mindful of them and giving them our undivided attention.

Like all texting-while-driving temptations, which should be locked away in the glove compartment before we even put our car in gear, when it comes to listening to others, our multitasking endeavors and our phone distractions should also be turned off and stowed so we can give our undivided attention and our full mind to others. No exceptions. Anything less is disrespect!

I can distinctly remember an incident, before the advent of message machines, when I was in my superior's office and his landline phone began to ring. I asked if he were going to answer it. He replied that who-ever it was could call back because it was far more important that he pay attention to me. That was mindful listening. And I've never forgotten how respected he made me feel.

Prayer is defined as talking with God, which includes listening. How often do we give our undistracted, un-multi-tasked, mindful attention to God when we pray?

HOLY HOMEWORK

Let's shut down our mobile phones and talk with God for fifteen unin-terrupted minutes. We might be surprised at what he has to tell us, if we are truly listening.

Angry in August

Are humans more irritable in the late days of summer than during other months of the year? The ancients certainly believed that the July and August rising temperatures caused an equal rising in tempers. The so-called "dog days" of summer made people and animals angry and wild.

Is this especially true for New York City dwellers? Maybe so! The close quarters and crushing crowds of a subway commute in mid-winter are certainly no cause for rejoicing. But add perspiration and broken air conditioning to the mix, and our patience, like our fuses, can shorten considerably when the humidity is suffocating.

Climate aside, how "Christian" are we when it comes to dealing with the deadly sin of anger, our own or others?

Solution number 1: Walk away, even if it's only for a jaunt around the block or just stepping back for a few seconds to take a deep breath and count to ten. This remedy works for both parties: the angry person, and the recipient of the anger. How can "retreating" be a noble resolution for anything? Wouldn't this be tantamount to avoidance? No. A temporary withdrawal does not mean sweeping the issue under a rug or pretending it doesn't exist. This recess is only a short separation.

What purpose does this reprieve serve? This brief "time out" gives the angry person a chance to cool off. After all, any strong emotion, particularly anger, clouds our judgment. So even when our anger is justified, we don't want to escalate our tension to the point of saying something we'll regret later.

The reason the receiver of another's anger should turn away is even simpler. It is impossible to argue with people who are angry because angry people believe they are right. How can we have a discussion with people who think they are correct and everyone else is wrong? We can't. So, it's best to postpone any dialogue until later on when the other person's anger has subsided and a "Christian" conversation is actually possible.

Solution number 2: Switch perspectives by peering through the other person's lenses for a while. Here is a little-known fact about our species. We cannot adopt another person's viewpoint and also be angry with that person. Humans are incapable of doing both at the same time. When we are mad at someone, as soon as we look at the world through their eyes, our anger diminishes.

Again, this practice works for both parties. The recipient should also try to envision what the irate person is seeing. Can we visualize an injustice when we take their point of view? Would we be just as frustrated and upset if our positions were reversed? And if so, can we realize why they might perceive their anger as justifiable?

Solution number 3: Recognize and respect where the other person is coming from.

More than anything, angry people want to feel understood. They want to know that someone else on the planet comprehends what they're going through. This does not necessarily mean "agreement." But it does mean acknowledging and appreciating their experience of the situation.

Solution number 4: Accept misplaced anger as a compliment rather than a threat.

Anger is a socially repugnant emotion. Such outbursts make adults appear childish and out of control. When an angry person gets "in our face," it is extremely difficult for us not to become hostile in return. However, we can remain calm if we accept the other person's anger as a compliment rather than a confrontation. This is no easy task. But if adults allow themselves to regress into a tantrum in our presence, this may say more about their placing trust in us rather than their being a threat to us.

Solution number 5: Pray, not as a last resort, but for continual support. Prayer works. And it works for two very good reasons. The first reason is supernatural. God exists. God hears our prayers and answers them by giving us the graces we need when we need them. The second reason is natural. When we pray, our concentration shifts from selfish to selfless. During prayer, we turn the spotlight away from ourselves and more toward God. As we ask God for assistance, we open our hearts to receive his help. Our focus becomes less and less on our pain and more and more on our power. Our confidence builds through our belief that the strength of God will bolster our weaknesses.

HOLY HOMEWORK

Let's pick a clammy day in the summer and allow a piece of paper to "stick" to our sweaty forearm. Then let's meditate for a moment by asking: How closely do we "stick" with God when we get irritable or when someone gets angry with us?

23

Simple, Safe, and Spiritual

In his infinite wisdom, God has ways of keeping us simple, humble. This is good. Otherwise, we might forget that we are the creatures, not the creator. God keeps us safe, trusting. He gives each of us a guardian angel to whisper in our ear about not texting while driving. If we ignore this angelic voice, we risk getting into an accident or getting a fine. God wants us to be good, spiritual. He thinks about us constantly. He has more pictures of us in his mind than any family photo album could hold. After all, we are made in his image and likeness.

Simplicity: Humble Pie

C. S. Lewis said humility is not thinking less of yourself but thinking of yourself less. I began teaching collegians when I was twenty-eight years old. Having earned three master's degrees before stepping into the classroom, I walked in feeling ten feet tall thinking only of myself and what a grand impression I would make. I emphatically announced that people in the United States could recall exactly where they were when they heard the news that President Kennedy had been shot. From the sea of blank stares, one brave student finally raised his hand and respectfully reminded me that he and his classmates were five years old when that assassination occurred. He said they could not remember where they were because they could hardly remember who they were, let alone who Kennedy was. He concluded with the inevitable undergraduate follow-up: "Will this be on the final exam?" I exited the room feeling two feet tall.

Safety: Locksmith? Why?

Growing up in a household of ten, everyone had chores. We washed and dried dishes by hand. We hung wet laundry on clotheslines to dry. We took turns feeding the dog and cleaning the parakeet's cage. And neither snow nor rain nor hot nor gloom of night could keep us from entering our crowded home because we never locked our doors! My folks did not lock the car and left the keys in the ignition. Why wouldn't they? The car was safe. The house was safe. We were safe. How many angels can fit on the head of a pin? I don't know, but somehow ten guardian angels found room among ten active people who learned to trust that these spirits of God would help keep our family together, sane, and safe.

Spirituality: The Not-So-Candid Camera

The core of truthfulness and of spirituality is doing the right thing, whether supervisors are watching us or not. How often is someone observing us today? On average, the image of every person in America is captured more than seventy-five times per day. This number jumps to 300 times daily for big-city dwellers. However, the fifty million folks visiting Times Square each year can choose from any of the 6,000 eyes that never blink along the Great White Way. Since surveillance is as omnipresent as God, what intelligent person would seriously consider behaving badly in this society? Has the video in the cloud made us a better convert or just better at being covert?

Have Bygone Days Really Gone By?

The old days were more than simpler times; they were sacred times. Can we admit that our talents and gifts come from God rather than from our exclusive creation? Do we acknowledge our guardian angels? Do we behave with integrity, witnessed or not? There is something sacred about being modest without self-deprecation. There is something sacred about trusting others without bolts and alarms. There is something sacred about being trustworthy without being monitored. Such sacredness is the measure of our relationship with God. Spirituality is not a part of the era when we are living. Spirituality is part of how we are living in any era. Holiness is not joined to *when* we are, but *who* we are. Mary is the exemplar of humble modesty, obedient trust, and Christian holiness. This month, let's ask Mary for her assistance in growing these virtues into *who* we are today.

HOLY HOMEWORK

Using her statue or picture, let's create a small shrine to Mary somewhere in our home for this month. In front of her image, place three index cards, one behind the other, each containing one of these phrases: Creative Humility, Angelic Trust, and Mirroring God's Image. In the morning, decide how to implement the virtue on display. In the evening, move the displayed card to the back of the pack to reveal the next of the three. In one month, we will have practiced each of the virtues of humility, trust and holiness ten times to become closer to Mary and her Son in our daily lives.

Altar of Debt
or Altar of Sacrifice?

What is money? Let's begin by saying what it is not. Money is not the root of all evil nor is it the source of all blessings. Singer/comedian Pearl Bailey once quipped, "I've had poor and I've had rich, and I'd rather be rich." Very few people would choose to be poor. Yes, it is true that God chose to have his only Son born into poverty rather than riches. However, this was not intended to send the message that poverty was a good thing but rather that wealth, like power, was not something to be grasped at.

So, what is money? Money is a substitute means for exchanging goods and services. And this substitution works only as long as the collateral behind that money continues to exist and to be of value. If the collateral backing any currency disappears or becomes worthless, then money becomes useless.

We should meditate often on the significance that money holds in our lives and the purpose that it serves. We can begin with our life goals. For example, are the goals we have in life driving the goals we have toward making money, or vice versa? I once asked two college freshmen about their goals in life. Their answers were exactly the same. They wanted to make lots of money. Only then would they pursue their true desires in life. One wanted to become an artist and the other's dream was to write music. Given the competition in the fine arts, it might be difficult to argue with their approach. But it certainly appears as though the tail was wagging the dog.

Spiritually and practically, there are two big dangers regarding money, and both involve the concept of debt. First, if we become a slave to making money for the sake of making money, then we become addicted to accumulating capital. In other words, we become in debt to the idea of gaining riches. Second, if we spend beyond our means, something that is easy to do with credit cards, we can fall into financial arrears very quickly. Either way, we end up worshiping at the altar of debt rather than at the altar of sacrifice.

The bottom line, for the sake of our souls, is that making money should always be viewed as a means to an end, not an end in itself. The end should never be making money but rather becoming closer to God by using the money we make to advance our unity with others and salvation for all.

HOLY HOMEWORK

Let's leave all credit cards, debit cards, and checkbooks at home for three days and pay for everything, including bus fares, gasoline, and tolls with cash. Then let's reflect on how easily we can find ourselves worshiping at the altar of debt instead of the altar of sacrifice.

Gratitude

Thank you, Lord,
for dying for us, rising for us,
and loving us forever.

Fair-Weather
Faith

No one likes a fair-weather friend. These people only know you when they want something. Who needs associates like that? We can easily build up resentment toward them and turn away from them the next time they ask for our help.

My grandfather had dozens of fair-weather friends. A native of Sicily, he sailed to this country with very few contacts but with a boatload of talent and good will. Among his many domestic crafts was his gift for brewing homemade wine. And yes, my mom was one of his daughters who actually crushed truckloads of grapes by stomping them into liquid form.

I can recall watching comedian Lucille Ball prancing around in just such a vat. I was disgusted at the thought of people producing food with their bare feet. My mom shook her head and explained that this was not how it was done. Purple ankles might be the fashion in a Hollywood sketch, but in their cellar she and her sisters wore sanitized boots. And she was quick to add that my grandfather had bushels of friends while the vintage was flowing. But as soon as the wine was gone, so were they. Fair-weather friends! Who needs them?

What about our friendship with the Lord? Is our relationship with God steadfast no matter what the forecast? Or do we suffer from fair-weather faith? Are we friends with God and faithful to his commandments only when we need him? Is it always the case that war and weakness and want fill church pews faster than peace and power and plenty?

And if this is so, is God affected by our lopsided loyalty? Is he offended because we only cry out to him when the waves of misfortune are cascading over the bow of our sinking ship? Does it always take a storm of adversity to drown our pride and rudder our behavior back toward the shores of heaven? Thankfully, God is faithful, even when we are not. He sent his only Son into the world to forgive sin.

Let's select a relative, acquaintance or coworker who tends to be a fair-weather friend. The next time the person asks for help, instead of resenting the one-sided relationship, let's welcome the person warmly and help. Replacing retaliation with reconciliation turns our own fair-weather faith into steadfast love for the Lord.

The *Mayflower* in Winter

When the Pilgrims first spied Plymouth on the horizon, what were they thinking? "Is anyone on board having second thoughts about the wisdom of this venture?" or, "By a show of hands, how many would vote to turn right around and sail back to Europe immediately?" or, "Why are we sailing on a ship named the *Mayflower* when the calendar isn't remotely close to May and there isn't a blooming flower anywhere in sight?"

Honestly, these weary travelers could have echoed the same words that John Paul II said on his first papal visit to the United States, also spoken in historic Massachusetts. I can remember standing for hours in the overcrowded Boston Common waiting for his arrival. Everyone was getting soaked to the skin by a relentless deluge of cold, stinging rain. When the Holy Father emerged from the motorcade, instead of beginning with the celebration of Mass, he proceeded to a microphone at the front of the stage, took a long look at the soggy band of believers and said, "We could have picked a better day."

In 1620, those 102 seekers of religious freedom could certainly have "picked a better day" as well. After spending more than two months on the open waters of the Atlantic, the only reception that greeted the Founders of the Feast was sickness, starvation, and death. The chill of late fall wrapped them more in misgivings than thanksgivings. Had they set sail months earlier, they may have had a tough voyage across the ocean, but they would also have had the summer growing season to store up food against the harsh New England snows. Now, with no time to fell trees or build even temporary shelters on land, they were forced to live aboard their rocking vessel, bunking close together beneath the thin timbers of the creaking, windswept deck.

Fifty percent of them never left that ship alive. When someone died, two sailors would row the body ashore under cover of night. They would offer a quick prayer for the deceased but leave the grave unmarked. They feared what they believed to be uneducated, uncivilized, wild Native Americans would unearth the remains and discover how quickly their numbers were decreasing and how weak their bodies were becoming. Ironically, a native who spoke English and taught the untrusting travelers how to fish in the local waters helped them survive in the New World.

The Pilgrims came to America seeking freedom of religion. What they found was a savior-friend with an open hand of welcome; a godsend who would nurse them through a winter of despair and sit with them the following autumn to celebrate their very first Thanksgiving meal.

HOLY HOMEWORK

During grace before Thanksgiving dinner this year, include a special prayer for Native Americans, the descendants of those who helped the Pilgrims live to see a better day—a day of religious freedom for all.

Taking Back Saints, Souls, and Gratitude

Macy's Thanksgiving Day Parade marches in the heart of New York City every November, with its big brass bands, airborne balloons, and Radio City Rockettes. A total of 8,000-plus participants prepare a path for the final float of the festival carrying an abundant Santa and his overweight sleigh. What is the objective? To officially usher in the holiday season of December, of course, and to remind parents that there are tons of toys, glimmering gifts, and super sales for the savvy shopper who is smart enough to spend money now and avoid the last-minute rush.

Two thousand years ago, no floats, fliers, nor 8,000 fans were around to prepare the way of the Lord. There was only the voice of John the Baptist crying in the desert. However, the price was right. And here's the financial phenomenon of forever! That price hasn't changed across the millennia: just repent and be baptized and you receive the gift of the Giver of life and access to the reward of eternal life.

Recently there have been a few advertisements on billboards, bumper stickers, and in the media pleading with us to keep Christ in Christmas. Perhaps it is time to rescue the saints, the souls, and Thanksgiving as well.

I recently taught my college students the origin of the word *Halloween*: All Hallows' Eve, the night before All Saints' Day. They thought I was making it up! They were far more familiar with the tricks involved in trick-or-treating. To my ears, some of the retaliations against neighbors who did not provide enough free candy bordered on actionable vandalism. Soap night, cabbage night, and TP night paled by comparison to the more than 130 arson fires that were set in one year alone. Torched for lack of a Tootsie Roll?

All Souls' Day has not fared much better, I'm sorry to say. Bringing flowers to the graves of our deceased loved ones has been replaced with online recipes for chocolate coffins, sugar skulls, and the bread of the dead. Preparing for two days devoted to honoring heavenly heroes and remembering the souls of our faithful departed seems to have drifted as far afield from Christianity as the marketable Mr. Claus has from the charitable St. Nick.

HOLY HOMEWORK

As we prepare to eat our cranberry-laced chow in front of the widescreen touchdowns this year, perhaps we could think of one significant way to rid All Saints' Eve of the goblins, All Souls' Day of the saccharine, restore gratitude to the generous natives who kept the Pilgrims from starving, and return a strand of finite straw to the crib of an Infinite Child.

28

Happy
Indebtedness Day

Deliberately Indebted

A renowned statesman used to borrow a book from his opponent's office library the day before their public debate. This self-imposed indebtedness then served to remind him to act civilly toward his adversary no matter how heated the next day's exchange might become.

When we borrow money, we are indebted by justice to repay the loan. Even if others give us a "free pass," at the very least we owe them a debt of gratitude. Depending on the circumstances, a simple "thanks" may fill the bill, but some sign of appreciation is always in order.

While many Americans today might not equate "Turkey Day" with being indebted, nevertheless this is exactly what the festivity represents. The rationale behind the establishment of Thanksgiving was to set aside a day to remember that we owe God our gratitude not only for a bountiful harvest but also for the many other blessings we receive throughout the entire year and every day of our lives.

Young Peoples' Gratitude

As happens each fall semester a few weeks before Thanksgiving, I asked my sixty-five undergrads to list three things they are thankful for. This year, I also asked them to list one thing they feared and one thing that brings them great joy in life. Not surprisingly, there was a positive correlation between what they appreciate most and what makes them most happy. Their top ten replies for gratitude were:

Parents and family, 21 percent
Friends, 16 percent
Education, 11 percent
Technology, 11 percent
Fun and partying 7 percent
Food and coffee, 6 percent
Money, 5 percent
Options for the future, 5 percent
Mobile phones, 4 percent
Good health, 4 percent

These top ten were followed by several ties for last place, which included gratitude for the gift of their life, for their safety, and for their professors. I was not so much surprised that teachers were last on the list as I was that we made the list at all!

Next, the young adults in this survey admitted to these top five fears:
Failure, 33 percent
Future joblessness, 21 percent
Loneliness, 9 percent
Having to become mature, 8 percent
Terrorism, war, and violence, 8 percent

Their top five sources of joy were:
Friends and family, 13 percent
Money and stability, 11 percent
Romance, 10 percent
Approval from others, 10 percent
Success, 5 percent

Finally, 3 percent divided the cause for their bliss among video games, surfing the internet, and alcohol.

Since this holiday was first celebrated in 1621 between the Plymouth settlers and the Wampanoag Native Americans, it seems the seminal reason of indebtedness has taken a back seat to colorful parades, stuffed turkeys, and pumpkin pies. And although the Pilgrims and Puritans may never have envisioned this feast to be an annual occurrence, their intention certainly was to give thanks to God and their neighbors for having survived their first winter in the new world.

Before we sit down to watch our favorite football match, we might ask ourselves what are we most grateful for nowadays.

HOLY HOMEWORK

Each night this month before going to sleep, let's think back over the day and recall three things for which we are grateful. In these instances, besides God, do specific individuals also come to mind? And are they people we are rightfully indebted to? If so, let's offer a special prayer to God on their behalf and in thanksgiving for the inspiration they have given us.

The Internet:
Freedom or Fettered?
Intimacy or Isolation?

Americans bask in liberty. We relish it. We demand it. We die for it. For centuries, we have not only inhaled independence into our own lungs, but we have also raised a golden torch to light the way for any tired, poor, huddled masses who yearn to breathe the fresh air of making their own choices instead of suffocating on the pollution of tyranny. This is one of the reasons why we so quickly embraced the internet. Anonymity augmented our self-determination.

The Thrill of Victory and Free to Be Whomever

In the original social media of cyberspace, we were no longer limited to being ourselves. We were free to become anyone we wanted to be. Behind the veil of obscurity, we could choose a new name, a new identity, a new height, weight, age, ethnicity, marital status, income, and anything else we wanted to be and no one would be the wiser. The secrecy of the computer screen was an American dream suddenly wide awake and universally available in every corner of the earth. Everyone in the world was at liberty to be anyone, anywhere, at any time. Raise the flag!

The Agony of Defeat and Surrender of Privacy

Is the internet still an electronic American dream today or has it become an abysmal global nightmare? Are our travels being served by GPS tracking or is the Cloud raining on our parade? American consumers now purchase more products online than in stores. But what is the cost of never getting lost when traveling? Has the convenience of shopping from home also brought an intruder into the house? Have we locked our front door but handed over the keys to the back door to savvy hackers who can peek into our parlor now that we have TV from a multitude of sources?

Matchmaker Replaced by a Mouse

Today, one out of every three weddings are marriages between couples who meet online, a fact which even surprised *eHarmony* CEO Neil Clark Warren. Most are professional people who prefer introductions through dating services because they have busy schedules and no desire to go to singles bars. Electronic selfies have replaced introductions by knowledgeable family members and trusted friends. Blind dates are passé. Now we are free to read about, contact, and view potential mates, or we can decline without offending them or ourselves or the cupid with the bow and arrow.

Restoration of Appropriate Distances

When our great-grandparents first spoke into a telephone receiver, without exception they would shout into the mouthpiece. Why? To their way of thinking the person on the other end of the line was miles away and therefore it was necessary to be loud to be heard. Before Alexander Bell's invention, conversations were mouth to ear. The ability to whisper and still be heard was indicative of the level of intimacy between two people in the same room. The fact that our youth prefer texting to talking could be interpreted as a restoration of the proper distance that should exist when a relationship is casual rather than close.

More Involved or More Isolated

In 1776, the rockets of freedom were bursting in the air people breathed, not over the airwaves. As a nation of progressive innovators and electronic wizards, we must ask ourselves this most telling question: Has the internet enhanced our love for freedom and patriotic connections or compromised our right to privacy and engendered isolation?

Enter a Catholic church and proceed to the ranks of candles that the faithful can light for a small offering. If the rack holds actual burning candles, let's offer a prayer of thanksgiving for the fire of freedom that burns in all American hearts. If the rack contains electronic candles, let's offer a prayer of thanksgiving for the love of ingenuity that burns in all American minds. And if the church has no candle racks, let's offer a prayer of thanksgiving for those who strive to lead others out of darkness and into the light of truth. In each instance, let's offer a prayer of thanksgiving so that God will continue to bless America.

MERRY CHRISTMAS

Whenever we give generously,
touch tenderly,
and love irrevocably,
Christ is born again.

Embracing Our
Christmas Ghosts

From the start of his classic *A Christmas Carol*, Charles Dickens' story insists that Jacob Marley is dead. Otherwise nothing wonderful would come of his story. At the heart of this wonderment are four ghosts: Marley himself and the three Christmas spirits: Past, Present, and Future. As we all know, Marley sends these three specters to his miserly business partner, Scrooge, to help him see the error of his selfish ways. But Ebenezer wants no part of this spiritual intervention. He even tries to reduce their impact by asking if all three can visit at the same time rather than disturbing his precious sleep at different hours during the night.

Like this tired curmudgeon, we also can close our eyes against the plight of our neighbors who are in need. We can curl up cozily with the stingy Scrooge inside us, echoing the same solutions he bellows: Are there no prisons? Are there no workhouses? Are there no laws? Are there no government programs?

This December, instead of silencing our internal, ethical voices, perhaps we can carry them to a religious service just as Bob Cratchit carries Tiny Tim to church on his shoulders. Unembarrassed by his disabled appearance, the crippled child believes it might be pleasant for fellow worshipers to remember upon Christmas Day the one who made lame beggars walk and blind people see. When we look at Christ in the manger, will we remember to open our hearts and hands to the poor?

Our worst temptation may be to utter the same excuse that the entrenched Ebenezer whines: I'm too old to change. I'm beyond hope. Go and redeem some younger creature.

In the long run, such apathy toward evil may be more dangerous to the human spirit than incessant complaining. At least people who grumble about injustice are aware of it and vocal against it rather than merely looking the other way or pretending it doesn't exist.

HOLY HOMEWORK

During the Advent season, we can read, rent, or watch a TV edition of the Dickens' tale. Then, far from ignoring the gifted ghosts who are challenging us to change, we can embrace their healing message by identifying one self-centered vice in our lives and resolving to exchange it for a virtue.

God bless us, everyone.

A December
Resolution
for the New Year

How many times in our lives have we been cautioned not to take our loved ones for granted? Yet how often have we realized their profound value only after it's too late, when they're gone?

In anticipation of writing the first column of the new year, I asked a friend what came to mind when he thought about the month of January. After clicking off the usual array of trying to keep New Year's resolutions, the bitter cold winter weather and having even more gifts to buy (his brother celebrates a birthday in January), he paused for a moment and then added something unique: discarded Christmas trees strewn by the sidewalks!

We've all seen them. They lie there on their sides waiting for the garbage truck to haul them off or the recycling crew to take them away, perhaps to turn them into some newspaper we'll read in the future.

Even the artificial trees, which we disassemble and restore in the attic along with our family heirlooms carefully wrapped in boxes labeled "Christmas ornaments," are rarely thought about again until next December.

This brief image of the taken-for-granted, easily dumped tree reminded me of how "conveniently" we can pack up the authentic spirit of Christmas by day 31 of December and keep it tucked away, collecting dust, or even worse, abandoned altogether for the next eleven months. And it also inspired an equally brief, albeit hopefully poignant poem about extending the holiday message into January and the months that follow.

Beyond the Seasonal Tree

Tree in our living room, Living-room Tree,
Seasonal guest, so delightful to see.
Eagerly waited for, all the year long,
Silent, but welcoming; lofty and strong.
Standing so tall and yet easy to reach,
Symbol of Heaven whose message you teach.

Faith: by the wood of the tree that you are.
Hope: by the light on your crown from a star.
Love: by the colorful gifts at your feet.
Life: by the crèche figurines that we greet.

Brief is your visit, so quickly you're gone.
Fill us with giving the whole new year long.

HOLY HOMEWORK

If our tree sheds, let's gather a few of the needles and place them in a saucer in the middle of the dining room table for the month of January. Each day, as we add a drop or two of water to the dish, let's resolve that December 31 will mark the continuing, not the ending, of our authentic Christmas spirit. And if our tree doesn't lose needles, we can add a bead of pine oil scent to the saucer instead. Happy New Year.

Christmas Cooing

Cultural myths abound. I recently heard a friend from New Jersey reiterate the urban legend about alligators swimming in the sewers of New York City. Balderdash! Any resident of the five boroughs can testify that a discarded reptile doesn't stand a chance of growing to adulthood against the army of rodents that lurk beneath our streets. But hearing that fable reminded me of another cultural myth, an ancient wives' tale, about newborn babies.

My mom once told me that when infants giggle and coo it's because they're talking with the angels. Apparently while these tots are still fresh from the hand of God they have a direct line of communication with the heavenly powers. Unfortunately, the clarity in this celestial connection diminishes with the passing of years on earth.

I had never given credence to this myth of the cooing babes. But recently I learned about a strange encounter between a couple's two children, their four-year-old, and their newborn.

On the day they took their newborn home from the hospital, these parents were eagerly waiting for their four-year-old to return from day care so they could introduce the siblings to one another. Eventually the four-year-old came dashing into the house shouting, "Where is the new baby?"

"Upstairs, asleep," whispered the parents. "Would you like to peek in?"

"Yes," gasped the youngster, finger over lips, imitating their hushed tones.

"We'll go with you," said the father.

"No," the child objected firmly. "Just me. By myself."

The parents looked at each other in disbelief. They weren't expecting such an odd demand. The mother was especially concerned because she had been reading about sibling rivalry and how a previously "only" child can become jealous when a newborn joins the family.

The husband noticed his wife's apprehension immediately. But he let his eyes dart back and forth from her gaze to the two-way monitor resting on the coffee table nearby. The reassuring expression on his face seemed to say, "Don't worry. We'll be able to hear everything that goes on in the nursery by listening through this wireless device."

The wife understood her husband's unspoken message and responded to the four-year-old in halting phrases. "OK," she announced reluctantly.

"But you must be very, very quiet. And you must not disturb the baby in any way. Do you understand?"

The youngster nodded and scampered to the top of the stairs in a flash. Just as quickly, the parents glued their ears to the mechanical monitor. They eavesdropped as the door to the nursery creaked open and shut. They held their breath as they listened to the tiptoed steps advancing steadily toward the crib. Then, ever so softly, they heard their elder child ask this favor of their newborn.

"Quick. Tell me about God. Tell me about God's love. I'm forgetting what his voice sounds like, inside me."

Cultural myths aside, we've all wrestled with our share of specters in life, some of our own making, some not. Perhaps the cries of religious disillusionment or the beckoning of secular distractions has deafened the summons of our innocent faith. If so, then we would benefit by listening carefully this month to the welcoming whispers of the Infant Savior born on Christmas Day. We may never know the secrets that newborns share with the angels. But our world would slumber in more peaceful, silent nights if we all welcomed the message of the Christ Child with open minds and open hearts. And in case we have begun to forget, we could ask the Baby Jesus to tell us again about the Father's love; to remind us of the sound of God's voice, calling from inside.

HOLY HOMEWORK

Find a quiet room to spend fifteen solitary, uninterrupted minutes, eyes closed, with some calming instrumental music, preferably a lullaby, in the background. Offer this time as an open invitation to hear again that heavenly voice you may have forgotten over the years. What would God say to us?

Christmas Gossip

Did you hear?

What?

She's pregnant.

No!

Yes. And, are you ready for this, she is going ahead with it!

Really? Even though she's not yet living with her husband?

That's what I heard.

How old is she?

Sixteen.

Her poor parents. What they must be going through.

Tell me about it.

I thought she was seeing whatshisname, that fellow who works with the lumber.

She is. In fact, they're betrothed. But he is not the father.

Is that right?

That's the word around the well.

Then he'll probably divorce her quietly?

On the contrary, they left town together this morning. Can you believe that?

Get outta here.

I don't know what has gotten into young people nowadays.

Hey, it's a modern world; a crazy, modern world.

This juicy piece of scandal was first circulated more than 2,000 years ago. The point in passing along such scuttlebutt today is simple. To quote Will Rogers, the renowned radio and stage star, "The only time people dislike gossip is when you gossip about them."

Rogers was right. Everyone savors a succulent slice of shame, as long as it's about somebody else. Of course, we wouldn't want any of our own indiscretions plastered across the walls of *Facebook*. But we don't want to miss any *Twitter* titillations either. Why? Inclusion. Gossip proclaims we've been included.

Think about this statistic. In a recent survey for organizational communication, people were asked what they found most gratifying about their employment. Can you guess what phenomenon generated the most contentment on the job? No, it was not flexible hours, nor better working conditions, nor even a salary increase. The number one source of job satisfaction was the feeling of "being in on things."

Apparently, for most Americans, the biggest setback at work is being left out of the loop. And although I have not seen any collateral studies, I would wager that such motivation is not confined to careers. Does anyone want to feel as though they've been kept in the dark in any context, whether at the office, in the neighborhood, at home or with friends? And what about at church? Besides the spirituality of their sanctuary worship, isn't one of the hallmarks of religious congregations the quality of their fellowship? This means that parishioners need to feel welcomed and included.

What we cannot escape during the season of Advent, as we prepare for the coming of Christ at Christmas, is the fact that Jesus and Mary and Joseph were isolated, rejected, and abandoned by their fellow human beings. Only the animals around the manger had the generosity to include them. And even some of those beasts may not have been thrilled about having to give up floor space and straw to accommodate three humans.

Must it always take an epiphany of angels to bring everyone, from shepherds to sultans, to their senses?

How inviting are we? How open are we? How eager are we to embrace the fullness of Christ and his message in our daily lives? Do we communicate the spirit of God's Incarnation to everyone we meet? Or is the true meaning of Christmas gathering dust amidst the silent statuary in the crèche beneath our holiday tree?

We began with a quote from Will Rogers on whispering about others behind their backs. What better way to conclude than with another quote about rumors from this very same humorist? He said, "Live so that you wouldn't be ashamed to sell the family parrot to the town gossip."

HOLY HOMEWORK

Instead of gossipy remarks, let's set aside a few minutes of family time this month to share constructive comments about other folks. We can start by saying three positive things about neighbors and extended family members who are not in the room. Then, to continue this spirit of inclusion, we can mention three appealing qualities about each person who is in the room. What better Christmas gift can we offer than endearing observations about the people we love?

Is Christmastime Family Time?

Before we can ask if Christmastime is family time, we need to define the word family. Naturally during the holidays most people think about relatives first. But friends, neighbors, and even a few business associates also figure into the festivities as well. Those who are not part of the family may receive an annual greeting card, a phone call, a visit, or even a tiny gift. The question is, who is part of our family and who is not?

I still exchange Christmas cards with friends and neighbors, even if email is rapidly eating into that industry. However, I've always been a little uneasy when vendors start sending very expensive gifts via parcel post. A token of appreciation is one thing, but when a poinsettia plant arrives that is so big it can't fit through the front door, then that contract labor may need some new bids. On the other hand, some of our regular helpers become like family members, don't they?

One of our New York newspapers once ran a full-page warning about how generous we should be when gifting these folks during Yuletide. For example, the nanny should receive at least one week's pay if not more, the doorman and the super a cool hundred each, and the mailman a bottle of wine. Yes, times have changed. When I was growing up, only the milkman received a treat on our back porch and that was from the same batch of homemade cookies that we left out for Santa.

So, who is our family? Recent research indicates that some modern attitudes toward family have changed considerably, while others have not. The best news is that most people feel as happy or happier with the family they have now compared to their family of origin, regardless of how it is defined. Over the past half-century, the primary shift in how younger generations choose to define the word *family* is not limited to one father and one mother with their own biological children. Nowadays, most people still define that traditional nucleus as a family, but many also include extended, blended, mixed and adoptive members, single parents and alternative lifestyle couples, provided they have children. For most responders, couples without kids fall outside the modern definition of family.

Each year in December, the Catholic Church celebrates the feast of the Holy Family on the Sunday between Christmas and New Year's Day. If

Christmas occurs on a Sunday, then the feast is celebrated on December 30. Somewhat ironically, we could say that the Church was 2,000 years ahead of its time, since the Holy Family was not a traditional family at all. Saint Joseph, as we know, was not the father of the Child Jesus but rather his foster father and a man who was willing to designate Mary as a single-parent mom if an angel had not intervened.

HOLY HOMEWORK

If you do not own one already, search for and download a free picture of the Holy Family and post it on the refrigerator during December. Then sometime during this month, preferably over a wholesome evening meal, discuss what the word *family* means to you and your loved ones.

Merry Christmas.

Our Favorite Christmas Present and Why

Most of us were blessed with a happy childhood. Even if times were tough back then, we still tend to look upon our youth with fondness. Perhaps this is because we were innocent. Or maybe our current recollections of the fun we had running and jumping simply outweigh the few tears we shed over a skinned knee or a scraped elbow. We sustained very few injuries that a soapy rinse, a dab of Mercurochrome, a bandage, and a kiss from Mom couldn't cure in a jiffy. Then we were outside playing again, racing bicycles and soaring on swings, as long as there was light in the sky. Any dark clouds that may have risen in our developmental history eventually fade into the shadows as the years blur by. Such "forgettings" and "forgivings" are among the graces of growing older and wiser.

"What are you hoping Santa will bring you?" and "What did you get for Christmas?" are two staple questions during the month of December. But these seem to be directed almost exclusively to kids. Adults get gifts that make their work easier. The larger microwave for Mom and more powerful snow blower for Dad can hardly be called toys, even if they come wrapped with a big red bow.

Have we ever asked our parents about their childhood? Have we ever wondered what was in their letter to the North Pole when they were growing up? Do we know which presents were their favorites and why? If we inquire, we might come away quite surprised by their response.

I once asked my mother about her favorite toys at Christmas. Her reply was both sobering and shocking. She grew up during the Great Depression, so there was no such thing as toys, as in plural. There was only one. This is how she recounted her Christmas morning. After returning home from an early Mass with her father, she would wait patiently as he fetched their wooden ladder and climbed to the attic. From there he retrieved a dust-covered shoebox, which he placed in her eagerly waiting hands and wished her a Merry Christmas. She gently unraveled the white tissue paper revealing her old baby doll, the same toy she received every year. The rest of the day was spent playing with, talking to and mothering that make-believe infant until dinnertime came and the gift was returned to the rafters.

Whatever sadness Mom may have felt as she watched her annual present repose to its rooftop mausoleum was replaced by her genuine anticipation for the next 25th of December, a scant twelve months away. She wasted no energy on regrets or resentments. Her focus was solely on her joy over her reunion with the doll and her gratitude for the eight hours they spent together. Honestly, I cannot recall which came as the biggest surprise to me: her having only one doll, her receiving that same doll year after year, or that she was only allowed to play with her doll for one day, but still felt completely content!

My own childhood arrived during a less stringent era. Baby boomers played with toys from Christmas day until we got bored or they got broken, whichever came first. My favorite gift each year was a new model to build, usually a car or a ship. The tiny parts and sticky decals provided a challenge to my fine motor skills and afforded me a proud display when the glue and paint was dry. My favorite was the intricate rigging on the tall sails of on a model of the HMS Bounty.

Are there any bridges here? Are there any universals that we can identify about Christmas gifts across generations? We can recognize a few. The Christmas present involves an extended period of waiting which results in a joyful presence when it finally appears. The Christmas present involves the seasonal reciprocity of giving and receiving. The Christmas present involves the Incarnation virtues of generosity and gratitude. Seen from this vantage point the true Christmas present really has not changed much in over two thousand years!

HOLY HOMEWORK

Let's begin by initiating a conversation with a parent or someone their age and asking them what their favorite Christmas present was when they were growing up. Then, let's display a picture of our favorite gift as a child or, if it hasn't been broken, post a "selfie" with it explaining why it was tops. Finally, let's spend a few prayerful moments exploring how presents in the past and presents today, though separated by years, still have much in common.

CPSIA information can be obtained
at www.ICGtesting.com
Printed in the USA
JSHW080056111122
32956JS00002B/11